BLASTOFF! READERS, AN IMPRINT OF BELLWETHER MEDIA BY FLUTTERBEE

Blastoff! Readers are carefully developed by literacy experts to build reading stamina and move students toward fluency by combining standards-based content with developmentally appropriate text.

Level 1 provides the most support through repetition of high-frequency words, light text, predictable sentence patterns, and strong visual support.

Level 2 offers early readers a bit more challenge through varied sentences, increased text load, and text-supportive special features.

Level 3 advances early-fluent readers toward fluency through increased text load, less reliance on photos, advancing concepts, longer sentences, and more complex special features.

★ **Blastoff! Universe**

Reading Level

This edition first published in 2026 by Bellwether Media, Inc.

For information regarding permission, write to Bellwether Media, Inc., Attention: Permissions Department, 3500 American Blvd W, Suite 150, Bloomington, MN 55431.

Library of Congress Cataloging-in-Publication Data is available at www.loc.gov or upon request from the publisher.

ISBN: 9798893047974 (hardcover)
ISBN: 9798893048971 (ebook)

Editor: Kieran Downs Designer: Brittany McIntosh

Printed in the United States of America, North Mankato, MN.

Table of Contents

What Are Sea Turtles?

Sea turtles are **reptiles**. They live in oceans around the world. There are seven different **species** of sea turtles.

Green Sea Turtle Report

Sea turtles have long **flippers**. Their front flippers push them forward through the water.

Their back flippers help them turn.

Most sea turtles have rounded heads and sharp **beaks**. Their eyes can see in water and on land.

Their heads and flippers are always outside their shells.

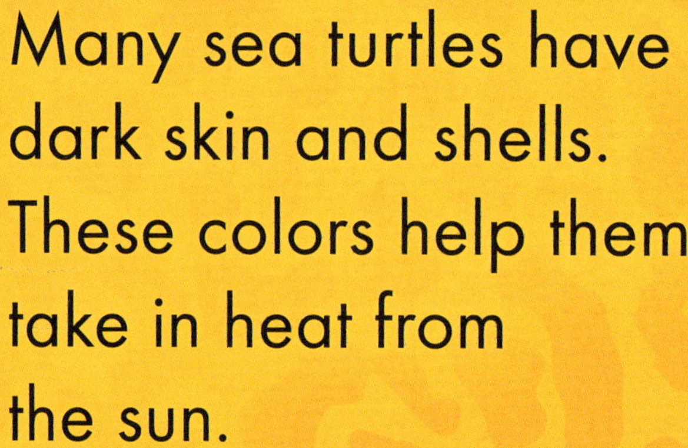

Many sea turtles have dark skin and shells. These colors help them take in heat from the sun.

Most sea turtles have **scutes** on their shells.

scutes

Spot a Sea Turtle
rounded head
shell
flippers

Single Swimmers

Sea turtles often live alone. They swim in **tropical** and **temperate** waters.

Many live near
coral reefs.
Some may go on land.

coral reef

Most sea turtles are **omnivores**. They **migrate** long distances to search for food.

Sea Turtle Food Web

sharks

jellyfish

seagrasses

algae

Some search for jellyfish and squids. Others eat seagrasses and algae.

Adult sea turtles are hunted by sharks.

shark

Sea turtles quickly swim away when danger is near. Many species have hard shells to stay safe.

Growing Up

Female sea turtles lay eggs on beaches. They dig deep nests.

Then they lay their eggs. Most can lay around 100 eggs at a time!

hatchling

The eggs **hatch** after about two months. The **hatchlings** then dig out of the nests.

They crawl toward the water.
Time to swim!

Life of a Sea Turtle

Name of Babies

hatchlings

Number of Eggs

around 100

Time Spent in Eggs

about 2 months

Life Span

Glossary

beaks—the mouths of some animals

coral reefs—groups of corals that grow in warm, shallow ocean waters

flippers—wide, flat body parts that are used for swimming

hatch—to break open

hatchlings—baby sea turtles

migrate—to travel from one place to another, often with the seasons

omnivores—animals that eat both plants and animals

reptiles—cold-blooded animals that have backbones and lay eggs

scutes—scales that cover the shells of sea turtles

species—kinds of an animal

temperate—related to a mild climate that does not have extreme heat or cold

tropical—related to places that are hot and humid

To Learn More

AT THE LIBRARY

Grack, Rachel. *Sea Turtles.* Minneapolis, Minn.: Bellwether Media, 2022.

Mather, Charis. *Discovering Coral Reefs.* Minneapolis, Minn.: Bearport, 2026.

Sabelko, Rebecca. *Ocean Animals.* Minneapolis, Minn.: Bellwether Media, 2023.

ON THE WEB

FACTSURFER

Factsurfer.com gives you a safe, fun way to find more information.

1. Go to www.factsurfer.com.
2. Enter "sea turtles" into the search box and click 🔍.
3. Select your book cover to see a list of related content.

Index

The images in this book are reproduced through the courtesy of: SeanScottPhotography, front cover (sea turtle); Vlad61, front cover, pp. 2-3; Mr.wutthiphat vimuktanont, p. 3; Bryan Chu, p. 4; DiveIvanov, p. 6; kaschibo, p. 7; Neil Aldridge, p. 8; Rich Carey, pp. 9, 10-11, 23; Kjeld Friis, p. 10; Gulf MG, p. 11; Seaphotoart/ Alamy Stock Photo, p. 12; Somphob Boonlaim, p. 13; Denisse Pohls, pp. 14-15; Matt9122, p. 15 (sharks); Aaronejbull87, pp. 15 (sea turtle), 17; Vladimir Wrangel, p. 15 (jellyfish); Damsea, p. 15 (seagrasses); abcphotosystem, p. 15 (algae); Wonderful Nature, p. 16; ymgerman, p. 18; Rainer von Brandis, pp. 18-19; Mesut Eksi, p. 20; Nimneth X, p. 21.